You Can Have it! It's Possible!

Healthy Relationships

How I learned to say goodbye to destructive relationships and say hello to the healthy ones.

FAYE HAYES SIMPSON

You Can Have it! It's Possible!

Healthy Relationships

How I learned to say goodbye to destructive relationships and say hello to the healthy ones.

Faye Hayes Simpson

T&J Publishers

A SMALL INDEPENDENT PUBLISHER WITH A BIG VOICE

Printed in the United States of America by
T&J Publishers (Atlanta, GA.)
www.TandJPublishers.com

© Copyright 2018 by Faye Hayes Simpson

All rights reserved. This book or parts thereof may not be reproduced in any form, stored in a retrieval system, or transmitted in any form by any means-electronic, mechanical, photocopy, recording, or otherwise-without prior written permission of the author, except as provided by United States of America copyright law.

ISBN: 978-1-7324905-2-9

To contact author, go to:
cfsimpson46@yahoo.com
Facebook: Faye Hayes Simpson
Linked In: Faye Simpson
Instagram: FayeSimp78

DEDICATIONS

First, I would like to thank my Lord and Savior, Jesus the Christ. Thank you God for loving me and teaching me how to love and build healthy relationships.

I also dedicate this book in memory of my brother, Barry Hayes (RIP), my nephew Tyreas Hayes, my niece Khisha/Khadijah Shalash (RIP). You all are truly missed and loved and will never be forgotten.

ACKNOWLEDGMENTS

I thank God for my mom and dad, Rosie Mae and Authur Hayes, Jr., who my siblings and I are still blessed to have in our lives. Thanks for teaching me how to be a lady, how to pray and keep my faith and trust in God Jehovah.

To my two sisters Darlene and Diana, I love you both. Thank you for reading and critiquing what I had written.

To my brothers Alfred, Marcus, and Rodney Hayes (aka Hollywood), I love you all.

To my daughters Kashawna and Aleshia Hayes as well as my son Cortez Barefield, thank you for being so wonderful and for encouraging me to get this book done.

I dare not mention my eight grandchildren: Ciara, Tyra, Stacey, Christian, Lauryn, Taylor, Roman and Keyivaun. You all are the joy of my life!

To Steven R. White and Adrienne D. White, you two are my wonderful pastors. Your constant prayers and words of encouragement to keep dreaming and striving for your dreams have kept me going. I remember when I first started writing and I had written quite a bit and I wanted Pastor Adrienne to read what I had written. She read it and handed it back to me and told me to write some more about myself so that people will know who I am and be able to relate to me better. Thank you for your advice.

A special thanks to a dear friend of mine, Terri Thurmond King. You spoke into my life some years back and told me that you saw me writing a book. Thank you.

To Alicia Payne Hill, who's an awesome author, I remember you had just published your book, *Woman Up*, and was having a book signing which I was attending. I approached you afterwards to talk to you and purchase your book. I told you I had started writing my book and was almost done. You said to me, "You know, there's more than one book in you," and that I didn't have to try and put everything in one book. After that conversation, you gave me your book for free. I will never forget those words of confirmation and encouragement and your act of generosity. Thank you.

To everyone I forgot to mention, thank you for your support, patience, understanding, and encouragement.

"Treasure your relationships, not your possessions."
—*Anthony J. D'Angelo*

Table of Contents

Introduction: You Can Have It...It's Possible!   11

Chapter One: My Upbringing   13

Chapter Two: The Breakup That Led To A Breakdown   21

Chapter Three: An Unexpected Loss   31

Chapter Four: Facing My Insecurities   41

Chapter Five: We Were Created For Love   51

Chapter Six: The Foundation Of A Healthy Relationship   57

Chapter Seven: Before You Jump Back In   73

Introduction
YOU CAN HAVE IT...IT'S POSSIBLE!

MY LOVE AND COMPASSION FOR PEOPLE, particularly, those who feel like outcasts, misfits, who feel overlooked and rejected, these are the ones I tend to be the most drawn to. My ability to be transparent has allowed those I've interacted with over the years to confide in me without fear of being shamed or judged. Why? Because I enjoy building relationships with others; and in order to do this, there are certain things we must consider and do.

Relationships can be complicated and difficult to build and maintain, especially if we don't know how to do so effectively. But over the years and through years of trial and error, I've discovered many of the tools that are necessary to build healthy relationships. For example, it's my belief that in order for anyone to be in a constructive and healthy relationship of any sort, communication is the key. There are many forms of communication: for example, there are verbal and nonverbal forms of communication. We communicate with our body language, facial expressions, tone of voice, etc. This is what determines how we'll be received by others. Relationships are developed and built on receiving and exchanging information. However, misjudging others before carefully examining them and becoming informed of who they are can lead to a lonely life's journey. You can have it...It's possible is a book designed to help us carefully look at the relationships in our lives. Health and wellness in our relationships are just as important as our physical health.

    In this book, I share my personal testimony and I also share some of the wisdom I've accumulated through my experiences with relationships of all kinds, romantic, family, and friendships. Whether married or divorce (I been there too), single or dating, or simply trying to deal with family drama, I'm here to let you know that there's always hope for a positive change. You don't have to settle for less than what God has predestined for you. It is possible! You can have it! Healthy Relationships. And I am here to show you how. Let's get started.

Chapter One
My Upbringing

I am one of seven siblings. I grew up in a house with two older brothers, two older sisters, and two younger brothers. I considered myself the baby of the family even though my brother, Hollywood, is three years younger than me. So really, I was just the baby girl. He liked to refer to me as his *baby sis*, which always made me chuckle. I wasn't your finicky, whiny type of girl; I was more of a tomboy. I was not spoiled and felt as if I had to have my way; we just had too many chores and other responsibilities that we had to do (unlike today's children).

My parents were born in Georgia. They always worked hard and would often talk about what all they had to do outside of their household chores. Even though they would share their stories about growing up in the South, I felt like they didn't understand my perspective when it came to things. I believe even though they didn't have much, they were happy. They looked forward to family dinners where everyone sat at the dining table and ate together. At Christmas, they were happy to get a bag of fruit or candy, maybe even a toy. My mom would tell us the story of her life growing up and end with a smile, telling us they had big fun. I just couldn't imagine going through some of the difficulties they faced growing up in that time. While she loved Georgia, mom decided to move us to Ohio in 1952, two years after the loss of my brother—he was my mom's firstborn. He died at eight months old from complications of double pneumonia. Maybe today he could have been saved, but treatments and technology weren't as advanced back then as they are now. I still remember my mom talking about the home remedies and concoctions my grandma would mix up. I couldn't help thinking from the sound of some of it, that it would either 'cure ya' or kill ya'!'

My grandparents were still living when my mom decided to move to Ohio. I'm sure that was a difficult decision for my mom to leave her parents and siblings—she had five siblings: three brothers and two sisters. My grandparents lived to be in their late 80s, and if my memory serves me right, they only came up to Ohio twice before they passed on. My grandpa was

Chapter 1: My Upbringing

a sporty man, always dressed to a tee. My grandma was a little lady, very petite, always in a sun-dress with her apron on. She loved to cook—she was a great cook. I'm sure that's where my mom got her cooking skills from. My mom told me she helped her mom prepare meals in the kitchen as a young girl. My dad's mom died when he was about seven-years-young and his father died a few years later. He quit school when he was in the eighth grade to help out and maintain the home he shared with his two sisters and one brother. I believe life as a young man who had lost his parents was very difficult for my dad because he was not able to receive the full effect of a mother's nurturing, affirming and loving touch. I say this because I believe that as a young man grows up, his mother is the first example of a woman and teaches him how to treat a woman with love, respect, and honor. As women, we know that when we have a good man we have *to be willing to help fill in the gaps and empty spaces and guide them into their role as priests.*

    In our home it was mom that laid down the house rules, and she didn't play! She had no tolerance for calling each other names, passing licks, swearing, teasing, or belittling one another. My mom hated lying. In her eyes, if you would lie, you would steal. My dad, on the other hand, was very quiet and laid back, but when he did talk, he'd talk so fast we could hardly understand what he was saying. I would be silly and try and imitate him, and I got caught one time and was put on punishment. We may have gotten by with a little more stuff with dad than with mom. She wasn't having it, so don't even try it!

My mom said, "Speaking don't hurt nobody. If someone says 'hello' or 'hi,' speak back and treat people the way you want to be treated." She always said things have a way of coming back on us. Mom taught us to use manners and to behave like we had good home-training, and she made sure we didn't embarrass her by being disrespectful or showing out in public. She would tell us, "Whenever and wherever you show out, that's where you will get disciplined." There was no waiting until we got home. Oh, no! You got it right then and there. And she said we had best not think about acting up in school. She told us that we were there to get an education and that the teachers had their education already. Mom said some of the teachers didn't care if we got our education or not—that only we would suffer the consequences for not getting our education. She told us if she had to come to the school-house because we were acting up, she was not going there to talk. Heaven forbid we were sassing or taken home by another parent, or we were disciplined by another adult—we would expect to get our behinds tore up! Yes, another parent was allowed to discipline us if we were misbehaving, especially if they knew our parents.

Chapter 1: My Upbringing

My mom loved to dress us girls up for school in dresses, ruffled socks, and patent leather shoes almost every day. We definitely weren't going to have one hair out of place. Me, being the tomboy I was, I hated wearing dresses. I would sometimes come home with my dress torn, dirty; just looking a mess. My mom would tear my tail up! A few more times coming home like that and she finally came to the conclusion that she wasn't going to dress me up for school like that anymore—only on Sundays and special occasions, of course. I was like, "Yes!"

Mom also talked to us about girls being jealous of other girls, little boys, dating. She told us while laughing—although we knew she wasn't joking around—that our books, pencils, and paper was our boyfriend. That's my momma. Mom spent time with us, teaching us how to cook, sew, and keep a clean house. We were raised with good morals and standards, something I feel is lacking in our society today. I realize we live in a time where a lot of things have changed and things are a whole lot different now than they were when my parents were growing up.

My mom told us life will bring its own share of problems without us creating them and she considered us her pride and joy. Both of my parents worked hard, but mom was the one who managed everything—paying bills, grocery shopping, washing, starching and ironing clothes, etc. She made sure we had what we needed. We were all in various sports and involved in a lot of activities. She would travel with us to every event that we had to attend. My dad would contribute financially as his way of showing support, but I don't recall him being at any of our games and events, and that may have been due to his work schedule. I do remember my dad always being at home in the evenings; and on Sundays, that was his day to take us roller skating, which he enjoyed doing and we looked forward to.

My mom would fuss sometimes about certain things; perhaps she felt like she had a lot on her shoulders. The tension and bickering between my parents would bother me, perhaps even more than it did my siblings. My dad never raised his voice. His disposition was quiet, reserved, and friendly like he could talk with anyone. He'd show very little reaction and response whenever mom would get uptight. I think that made her even madder. My mom and I are very similar, but I have some of my dad's personality as well. I like to think of myself as caring, outgoing, reserved, and friendly, a peacemaker, someone who will have your back, and someone that doesn't like drama.

I guess you can say I was more of a daddy's girl. I can remember my dad teaching me how to cut floor tile and carpet. My dad worked in the furniture business for years, and when my brothers weren't around to help he asked me to help him lift and move furni-

Chapter 1: My Upbringing

ture. I must say, I was pretty good at it, too. My mom made a comment to my dad one day: "You think she's a boy! Where them boys at, can't they help you move some furniture?" My dad's response was,

"They're never around when I need them! She's strong for a little girl. I'm not going to let her get hurt." We had to change our school clothes and do chores before we could go outside and play. I don't recall us having as much homework as children have today. We also had to go to church growing up; that was not an option. I was very involved at the church I attended, singing in the choir, children's band, etc. I developed a relationship with the Lord at an early age. I learned how to pray and study the Bible. I was trying my best to hold onto that even while I felt I was slowly but surely straying away.

YOU CAN HAVE IT! IT'S POSSIBLE! HEALTHY RELATIONSHIPS

Chapter Two
THE BREAKUP THAT LED TO A BREAKDOWN

I BEGAN REBELLING AROUND THE AGE OF fourteen. There seemed to be a lot of confusion going on. I wondered what happened to being kind and considerate of one another's feelings. I started hanging out with my friends, smoking cigarettes, and skipping school. The people I hung around with had other people that they associated with that also smoked weed, marijuana, reefer, pot, whatever you want to call it, but I tried it and then decided that it wasn't for me. I didn't like being paranoid, laughing at stuff that really wasn't funny, and having the munchies and craving everything in the refrigerator. I also got into a few fights. I had four brothers, so I learned how to protect myself. I wasn't a bully, nor did I pick fights. I wasn't a troublemaker. My mom finally asked me, "Child, what's going on with you?" She told me I better get my attitude together and she asked if there was something I needed or wanted to talk to her about. My mom said she noticed that I had been hanging out with different people, and not my usual friends. My parents didn't allow us to just hang out with just anyone. They would often say, "Don't let the company you keep get you into something that they may not be able to get you out of." She asked if that's why I was being so unruly. Our personalities sometimes clashed. My mom tended to be very outspoken, direct, and straightforward, and so was I. We both believed in speaking our mind; however, I didn't believe in back talking because I knew better. I didn't have an answer to her questions about my behavior. I had a feeling that my family didn't really understand me; and looking back, I'm not so sure if I understood me. I would try to voice my opinions without being disrespectful, but everything I would say would be taken that way; so I began keeping my thoughts and feelings to myself.

  My mom began regulating a few things to keep the peace and love that unified us as a family. While I was still acting up at home, I did clean up my act a little bit at school. I'd do all of my homework assignments in study hall just so I could hang out as late as

Chapter 2: The Breakup That Led To A Breakdown

I was allowed to when I got home. I stopped hanging out with some of the people I use to be around.

One day, when I was walking home from school, I met someone who I grew to like very much. He said, "Hey college girl, what's your name?" I kind of laughed and responded,

"I'm in high school. My name is Faye."

The next day he was working on a house two houses down the street from where I lived. I just got in from school and was about to open the gate when he yelled my name. I said hi, and he asked if I had a good day at school. I said yes. We talked for a little bit and then exchanged numbers. He seemed to be my way of escape from what I thought was a messed up situation at home. He was older than me and we spent a lot of time together. We would talk for hours on the phone and my mom would ask, "Who you on that phone with all the time?" I would say a friend of mine from school. I was allowed to go with my friends as long as I checked in and came home by my curfew. My mom didn't find out about him until four or five months later. She, of course, didn't approve of him and wanted us to stop seeing each other until I had graduated. I was upset and angry because I really liked him and he treated me like a queen. My feelings for him were too strong to simply turn off. I did tell him what my mom had said, but we continued to sneak around anyway.

I was trying to make sure that my lack of interest in school wasn't that obvious by not skipping as much. I knew that concerned my mom. She was scared that dating would deter my interest in school, and she was afraid of me having a child before I was ready. I still wasn't spending a lot of time at home unless I was grounded or on punishment. My mom and I butt heads often. Finally, I thought "I've had enough!" I decided to run away. I was gone for about three months or so before my parents got a tip on where I was. I already had unruly charges against me. Well, needless to say, I was sent away. I had no choice but to accept and deal with what I had obviously brought on myself. I became very bitter and resentful. I didn't want my mom or anyone else to visit me. There were a lot of questions I was asking myself about my mom: 'How can you say you love me when you sent me away? What happened to being kind and loving, treating people the way you want to be treated?' Those words suddenly had no meaning to me. I learned how not to trust family or anyone; after all, in my mind, they were the ones who hurt me. I remember thinking I must be adopted. I can recall my mom, brother, and my cousin coming to visit me at CSC in Columbus where I was sent. I was told I had visitors by one of the ladies that worked at the facility. I asked who the visitors were. When I was told who they were I responded by saying I didn't want to come down and visit. The lady that was in charge of my dorm looked very shocked and

Chapter 2: The Breakup That Led To A Breakdown

she began talking to me. She said, "Your family drove all this way to see you and you don't want to see them? I'm going to give you some time to think about it and I'll be back." I was caught up in my feelings, and when I finally agreed to visit with them I only had fifteen minutes left for my visit. It was a very awkward visit. My mom asked me how I was doing. I said that I was okay. I think that was the extent of my conversation with her. I talked with my brother while my mom and cousin talked. The visit was finally over and we said our goodbyes.

I had six months to think about my actions and how selfish I had been. I knew that I had caused my parents a lot of grief and pain. I remember my mom telling me how worried she and my dad were about me. They told me while they were watching the news that it had been reported that a young girl around my age had been found dead. My parents said they were praying that that wasn't me.

I felt like no one heard my silent cry. I didn't know how to process all the things that were bothering me, so I guess I acted out. It was time for me to come home and I couldn't wait to kick it with my friends and my family. Mind you, I hadn't had a heart-to-heart with my mom, so I still had forgiveness issues to deal with.

I was back home. I would get up around 9 in the morning take, a shower, get dressed, eat breakfast, make sure everything was done, and leave out to enjoy my day. A couple of weeks went by and mom asked if I resented her since all I would do was leave early and go home before bedtime at around 9 or 10 p.m. I told her "of course not," still trying to avoid having that much-needed conversation.

    I stayed in touch with the guy I was dating when I got sent away. I wasn't sure if it was fair to hold him to a commitment with me or not. I hoped that he was not messing around or cheating on me. I heard that he had gotten involved with a young lady and I couldn't wait to confront him about it. We had said in the beginning of our relationship that if either one of us got involved with someone else while we were together it would be over between us. The time had come when I had some alone time with my boyfriend. I did question him about the young lady he was supposed to have been involved with. He didn't quite admit to it and there was a brief moment of silence. I didn't want to push it, so we just continued to enjoy one another's company and our time together. I couldn't just brush it off while we were talking and having a good time. He finally decided to admit that he had gotten involved with this young lady and that she told him that she was pregnant. We had what I thought was a very mature conversation, and even though I was hurt, I decided I wasn't going to compete with that, so I broke it off. I had all of these emotions and feelings piling on

Chapter 2: The Breakup That Led To A Breakdown

top of each other that I had not dealt with and didn't know how to release.

I would hang out with my friends after that, and while out, I would occasionally see my ex-boyfriend. We were always polite and cordial to one another even after the fact. During the time I was sent away, most of my friends were in steady relationships.

I began to withdraw to the point where I wasn't as outgoing and willing to do fun things like I used to. I began staying in and having my friends come to the house. I started noticing that I was changing in a way that was not me. I was becoming forgetful of dates, days, times; it was really strange. I eventually had a nervous breakdown that caused me to be hospitalized and put on medication. My ex-boyfriend would come by to visit me at the hospital quite often. Needless to say, I thought that was kind of odd. Maybe he felt guilty and partly responsible for my condition. He'd often say "I'm so sorry. I never meant to hurt you." I could only respond by saying,

"But you did."

My long road to recovery consisted of me seeing a psychologist on a regular basis. I learned during one of my sessions that I had some people I needed to forgive; I also learned I had to have a positive outlet. I was told by the psychologist that it's never good to bottle up your feelings. He said, "Even if you can't express what it is to whom you need to, write down exactly the way you feel first." I began to express my feelings whenever I felt like it was necessary. I still wanted to be nice and considerate and avoid being so offensive by being too direct, but I knew I couldn't hold things in. I still found this difficult to do. I think because I was trying to spare other's feelings even while being offended myself, and this caused others to not take my feelings into consideration. Eventually, I grew comfortable once more with speaking my mind; and all of a sudden, I'm smart mouthed; everyone felt like they couldn't talk to me without me going off. This was all because I'd learned how to speak up and express what was on my mind without feeling guilty and like I didn't have a right to voice my opinion. It was okay when they were saying whatever they wanted to me; but now that I have something to say back, they can't take it.

I finally had that heart-to-heart with my mom— it was long overdue. I also had a run in with my ex-boyfriend, but this time I needed to forgive him as well. I know what you're thinking, 'What, he did you wrong?' I learned after we had talked that the baby had been born and he was doing his part as a father, but the relationship wasn't working out and they had recently broken up. We eventually ended up back together. So he had one child and one soon to be born. My oldest wasn't his child although he kept asking me if she was. It was ironic that his oldest and my oldest

Chapter 2: The Breakup That Led To A Breakdown

are the same age. I had gotten pregnant with my first-born during our break up. I had just turned eighteen and graduated from high school, literally! I graduated June 5th and she was born the next day, June 6th. I was still living at home. I decided about six months later to enroll in a college and I began attending classes shortly after.

My mom and sisters were such a great help. They took care of my child while I was busy with school. It was exciting to them to have a grand-baby in the home since my two older brothers no longer lived in the State of Ohio. My daughter brought a lot of joy to the family. They spoiled her rotten. *My, oh my, how time flies by.*

You Can Have It! It's Possible! Healthy Relationships

Chapter Three
AN UNEXPECTED LOSS

MY BOYFRIEND AND I WERE STARTING TO GET serious again and I was going to graduate soon. I was getting assistance from the government and felt it was time for me to start making some preparations to move out and get my own apartment, when I found out I was expecting. I had also re-dedicated my life back to the Lord. My boyfriend started to take an interest in learning about God, attending church, and becoming a Christian. We wanted to do the right thing, so he would periodically go to church with me and we would often talk about the word of God. We were truly in love with each other beforehand, but our newfound love for the Lord made our love for one another become even more intense; we now felt inseparable.

In November, my boyfriend decided he wanted to go out of town and visit his grandma for Thanksgiving. I had a doctor's appointment to see how the baby was doing since I was close to my delivery date, which was December 20th. I told the doctor that he was off, and that my daughter should be born late November or the first week in December at the latest. I decided to stay home and let my boyfriend go to see his grandma. It was a week before Thanksgiving and he had arrived in Alabama a few nights before the holiday. I couldn't help but think, if our child wasn't going to be born until late December then I just may have to fly down there so she could be born in Alabama.

I was feeling good about everything. We seemed to be in a good place in our relationship. It had been two days and I hadn't talked to him since I let him know that my doctor visit had gone well and the baby and I were doing well. I thought about giving him a call, but time had gotten away from me—it was around 11:30 p.m. and I dared not call his grandma's house that late. I remember not being able to sleep, so I watched television until it got snowy. I guess there was nothing else on TV to watch. I just wanted to talk to my boyfriend. I eventually dozed off to sleep, but then I woke up at around 6:30 a.m. My sister was getting ready for work. We started talking and she was asking me if I was ready for the baby to come and how

Chapter 3: An Unexpected Loss

the relationship was going since me and my boyfriend got back together. I told her it was going well and that we were excited for our daughter to come.

My sister's boyfriend and my boyfriend were really good friends, almost like brothers. There were a few times in our conversation that some of the questions my sister was asking had me a little puzzled. She asked what I would do if we broke up again or something happened to him. She told me she always believed that we really did love each other. I told her we talked about just about everything, even death. I remember saying I'd probably lose it and jump into the casket with him. I don't know why my sister was asking such strange questions. Suddenly, my dad yelled upstairs, "Faye! I need you to come downstairs for a minute." I looked at my sister and asked,

"What does dad want this early in the morning?" She told me I better get up and find out what he wanted. I went downstairs and my mom told me she had some bad news. She then told me that my boyfriend, the father of my unborn child, had just been murdered, and I started yelling and screaming, "It ain't true! You're lying! You didn't want us together!" Finally, my mom had to give me something just to calm me down and get me to relax. I recalled my conversation with my sister and realized she knew all along—and she probably knew I wasn't going to handle it all that well.

I slept for a while. Whatever my mom gave me, it knocked me out. I was still in disbelief, so I decided to walk down to my boyfriend's mother's house. My mom didn't think I should go even though it wasn't that far— it was dark and kind of late, but I went anyway. I got to his mother's house and it was already crowded with people. Everyone was sitting around talking and I could feel and see sadness in the room. His sister came towards me crying and just hugged me. I still didn't want to accept it. I kept thinking I must have been having a bad dream and was sleep walking at the moment. I stayed maybe an hour or so before deciding to go back home. There were just too many people there and I was starting to feel overwhelmed. His sister gave me a ride home. My mom was up waiting for me when I got home. She asked me if they were going to fly him back to have his home-going service and I told her they were going to. It was very late, so I went upstairs to go to bed. My sister was sleeping, so I quietly got into my pajamas. I had been laying there for a little while, thinking, 'My life seemed to be finally moving in the right direction, now I get the news that the father of our unborn child had just gotten murdered while he was out of town visiting with his relatives.' I found out that he was a victim of mistaken identity.

I recall feeling shocked, devastated, and heart-broken when, all of a sudden, I started having con-

Chapter 3: An Unexpected Loss

tractions. I began making groaning sounds that woke my sister up. She arose and asked, "Hey, you okay over there?" She got up, turned the light on, and saw that I was in a lot of pain. She immediately got dressed and ran downstairs to tell my mom that she thought I was in labor. My mom rushed upstairs to help me. My sister attempted to put my shoes on me, but my feet were tensing up from the pain. She and mom got me into the car and we drove me to the hospital. I was checked into a room pretty quickly. Once examined, I discovered I had only dilated two centimeters. My sister took my mom home around 6 a.m. and then returned around 1 p.m. I remained at the hospital from 12:30 a.m. until 3:30 p.m. The doctor decided that I was in false labor and allowed me to go home. My mom was concerned about me. She wanted to know if I was going to go to the funeral in two days. I said,

"Yes, ma'am." I had to go—I needed closure.

His family had a home-going service for him in Alabama and then they flew him home to have a service for him in Hamilton where he was loved and well known. The day of the home-going service had arrived and I didn't know what to expect nor did I realize how big of an effect this was going to have on me in my condition. I went into labor that night after attending the home-going service. I was taken to the hospital when I started having complications. I didn't want to get upset or cry too much because I thought

35

this would somehow hurt my baby. I was trying not to be too emotional; so there I went, turning my feelings inward, something I'd grown good at whenever I feared letting my real feelings show. The reality that my daughter's father wouldn't get to see or know her and he couldn't be there to see her be born, all of these thoughts raced through my mind as I just laid there in a ton of mental and physical pain. As we say, "It just got real!" My blood pressure started escalating, almost reaching stroke level. I realized my holding back my emotions was doing more harm than good. The nurse pulled my mom outside of my room and began asking her questions as to why my blood pressure was going so high. The nurse stated that in her records from me giving birth in the past, there was no documentation about me having high blood pressure. My mom began explaining to the nurse about what had happened regarding the father of the baby. The nurse re-entered the room and spoke very calmly and softly, gently rubbing my back, assuring me that it was okay for me to cry, that she was aware of the circumstances. I began crying and crying and crying, and all of a sudden my blood pressure started going down. My daughter was born shortly afterward a healthy 7lbs and 8 ounces on November 27th.

    I was faced with the fear of being a single mother of two, going back to college, and being busy with work and school while trying to make a life for us. I

Chapter 3: An Unexpected Loss

had finally gotten my own apartment. I seemed to be growing up so fast and with so many responsibilities. I managed to maintain, trying not to repeat any of my old behaviors. I didn't want my children picking up any of my bad habits. I don't necessarily regret the path that I chose, but *I understand that the road didn't have to be such a bumpy ride—there might have been an easier route I could have taken*. I believe we live and learn; and the longer we live, the more we learn.

I had been praying and reading the Bible. I wasn't attending church regularly like I used to. I began to look and see things differently. I realized that I was responsible for my own choices and the decisions I had made. I had to accept the consequences of my actions. My decisions didn't just affect me, but everyone who loved and cared about me.

I had to acknowledge that I was mad at my parents but that I had no right to hold on to this anger. It's okay to feel a certain way whenever a situation arises or a circumstance occurs in your life that causes inappropriate behavior that is totally out of your character. There's a reason why those feelings are there. But to ignore them or act like they're not there or like you don't have a right to feel a certain way only creates a more serious problem like it did in my case. Own up to the way you feel. Don't suppress your thoughts, feelings and emotions. Just deal with them when they come in the appropriate way.

I now know I should have been able to share and openly communicate my feelings with my parents. I also realize that it's not fair to assume that others should automatically know what's bothering us if we choose to shut them out, especially after we've become pretty skilled at putting up a front. We only show and tell and allow people to see what we want them to based on what kind of affirmation, validation, approval, or acceptance we need at the time. I didn't take into consideration what my mom may have been dealing with: all of us kids, working, her own responsibilities as a wife, the added stress of a rebellious child, and any other worries or concerns she may have had that we were not aware of. It is very easy to assume something is one way when it's not or to blame others for our mistakes.

I discovered after having a family of my own that we, as parents, don't always know what to say or do when certain situations arise. Things have a way of catching us off guard and by surprise. We do what we feel and think is right at the moment and what we believe is in the best interest of our children. I used to say there's no parent manual that we can just pick up that says when x, y, and z happens turn to this page. We live and learn, usually through trial and error. But through prayer, we have the best guide in the universe to help us in this process: we have the Holy Spirit. God was teaching me how to be a parent while healing

CHAPTER 3: AN UNEXPECTED LOSS

my heart of the pain of my past. He had to bring me face to face with all of my insecurities, fears, and unresolved issues.

Chapter Four
FACING MY INSECURITIES

I NOW HAD THREE CHILDREN AND THEY WERE the joy of my life. I can remember when I was working I would only allow certain people to babysit my children. I mostly preferred those who were close in age to my parents. I was very particular about my children, some would say overprotective. I would often say, 'Lord please don't let anyone do anything to hurt or harm my children in any way or I'm going to jail.'

Growing up, our family wasn't the hugging, kissing type. I didn't want my children to question my love for them, so I would often give those hugs and kisses to them. I could tell when they were upset or if something was bothering them. I called it a mother's instinct. I had a time set aside for family discussions, this was my way of letting them know that they could talk to me about anything—and I meant anything!

I had decided to go out with some friends one night just to have a little fun and a change of pace since it had been about eight months or so since I had done anything other than work, go to school, and be a mommy. I was really enjoying myself and having a good time. My friends met up with their boyfriends and decided to leave, which was cool! I hung out for a little while before deciding to leave when I ran into my oldest daughter's dad. I was sitting there chillin' all by myself when he approached me. He asked if I was okay and wondered what was I doing there all by myself. I told him that I was out with some friends but they had left not too long ago. I guess he was trying to win me back from the first time we met, which was during the time I had gotten pregnant. I must be honest, we weren't together long before *she* was born. My oldest daughter was conceived during the time I had broken it off with my boyfriend after I got out of CSC. I had no contact with my oldest daughter's father shortly after the fact because he was arrested a week later. He was gone for a long period of time before she got to know or meet her dad. I was only intimate with her dad that one time and really didn't expect him to be the father. I know it's a little confusing, but I guess that's due to being a little under the influence and thinking at least it wasn't someone I didn't know. I know he asked if he could walk me home and I believed he was really trying to be a gentleman about it. Perhaps, one thing led to another. Perhaps, I was just in a vulnerable state and was like 'What the heck.' Yes, I was definitely a trip back in a day, but I wasn't into loose living and giving it up to every Tom, Dick, and Harry so-to-speak! I didn't do a lot of dating. If I was in a relationship with someone, I was all in for as long as it lasted.

My oldest daughter's father and I ended up back together. We stayed together for a little over a year, then I then had our son. He became controlling and aggressive at times, trying to keep me from my family and friends. I decided that I wasn't going to put up with that and that was the end of that relationship. He, of course, wasn't too happy about it and he tried to make it difficult for me to the point where I had to take out a restraining order against him.

I still had a few months left before I was finished with school, so I regained my focus and decided to really buckle down and concentrate on my priorities. I was so determined to finish school I wasn't interested in going out or hanging out with anyone even when I had some free time to do so.

It was finally time for me to graduate when my cousin decided that she wanted to play matchmaker.

She introduced me to this guy who I thought looked familiar. He was nice and a little nerdy. I then remembered that I would see him on the city bus that I'd take to the plaza. We'd speak briefly whenever we got on the bus, but that was it. We were both attending college at different locations, and since I was about to graduate I didn't want to get together with him, not at the moment; but we did occasionally go out on the weekends. We eventually ended up getting together, dating for about nine months, and then we decided to get married. I was twenty-seven years old when I got married. My son was five years old and since his biological father and I hadn't been together for some years, it seemed like the right thing to do at the time; the timing felt just right.

My husband at the time was a very smart man. He was employed with the Hamilton City Schools and the City of Hamilton Utility Department. He was very good with the children and very adamant about them getting an education and keeping track of their learning progress. We were a few years into the marriage when he got himself tangled up with substance abuse, but he was never abusive towards me or my children. I didn't really know how to deal with it. I was very involved with my church. I believe that is what became the source of my strength and peace.

I thought, 'All this time I've managed to protect and care for them to the best of my ability, now what

Chapter 4: Facing My Insecurities

have I exposed them to?' As a woman of faith, knowing what the Bible says about divorce, I felt trapped. I also felt ashamed and embarrassed. My business was out there—everyone knew my husband was on drugs. I tried to keep what was going on between us away from the children by maintaining all of the household expenses whenever he decided to blow his paycheck. I also tried not to lose my temper and go off on him in front of the children. One day, my son brought something to my attention. He said, "Mom I saw dad when I was walking home from school, but it was like he was hiding and didn't want me to see him." I sat down with my children during our family discussion time and decided that it was time to tell them what was going on. I gave them a few moments to absorb what I explained to them and I assured them that they could be honest about how they felt about it. My children began to express how they felt about their step-dad openly and honestly. They told me they loved him, but they didn't like what he was doing to himself. I didn't want them hearing about him from the streets and I wanted them to know their feelings mattered. I never worried about my husband mistreating or abusing my children. I think I made myself very clear in the beginning about how much my children meant to me and how if anyone tried to do them harm I would be going to jail. But I think that was the first time they ever saw me sad, angry, or crying. Remember, I learned how to suppress my feelings as a teenager. I can recall my oldest daughter saying,

"Mom, even though you try not to let us see you upset, we know you are." I wanted them to focus on being kids; after all, this wasn't their problem to deal with. I realized that I wasn't teaching them that it's okay to cry, to be sad, angry, and even happy or excited. They needed to know that these were—and are—natural emotions. I didn't want them to be afraid to express themselves and begin holding in and bottling up their feelings like I did.

I believe that the issues and insecurities as a teenager I refused to deal with are what caused me to stay in the marriage longer than I should have. I, however, continued to stay very active in my church, doing whatever I could whenever I could. It was my faith in God, along with a lot of fasting and prayer, that sustained me and helped me to maintain my sanity.

My children are everything to me and I certainly didn't want them to believe that they had to accept or put up with what I did. I endeavored to instill in them the instinct to look for certain things (characteristics, habits, etc.) whenever they decided to date. As parents, we tend to tell our children about the things we went through in hopes that they won't experience them also. We went through some stuff not knowing we were going to experience what we did; but since we did, we now tell them so that they don't have to. We

Chapter 4: Facing My Insecurities

have to be honest with our children when sharing our experiences and some of the things we endured that made our lives a little more complicated. I do think we need to be careful about how much information we share and how detailed we are with this information. I believe that when we are advising and instructing our children about the choices they make, wise or foolish, they need to know there are consequences.

The fact that my mom approved of my ex left me wondering and questioning if that's why I became an enabler or felt somewhat obligated. Nevertheless, I only hoped and prayed that the family discussions and home Bible studies gave my children an outlet and a strong foundation to stand on whenever they would be faced with disappointment, adversities, or opposition. I didn't want them to use not having a good father figure as an excuse. You can say my children were spoiled, but not necessarily with things; they were spoiled with a whole lot of love and attention.

My children's father wasn't involved in their lives throughout their entire childhood, which I felt left a lot of pressure on me. I do believe that the father's role in the home makes a very significant difference and does make an impact on the children. However, I believed that if my children became wild and out of control—as unruly as I was at their age—that I'd be the one labeled unfit and be called an irresponsible parent.

I can remember being so excited when I finally

graduated because my daughter was born the day after her father was murdered, literally. I knew I wanted to go to beauty school, so I enrolled in one a few months after my daughter was born. I had to encourage myself because many days I felt like a disappointment to my mom. I eventually got a job that helped me to pay my way through school. I graduated and received my Managing license in Cosmetology. I had set very high expectations for myself. I wanted to show my children that you will make some mistakes, but you don't have to let those mistakes stop you from setting and reaching your goals and dreams in life. I'd tell my children, "Whether or not you get the support you think you need, continue to strive and believe in yourself."

I had some challenging times when my children became teenagers. They, like all other teenagers, tried to be sneaky. I'd give them a curfew; they'd brake it. I'd put them on punishment; they run away from home. You name it, it happened. During those time, you reflect back on the things you put your own parents through. You find yourself walking the floor at night, praying and talking to God like momma used to.

We are sometimes accused of not parenting our children correctly, hearing others make comments such as, "They don't have any home training." While that may be true in some instances, that is not always the case. In all our efforts to raise our children with good morals and standards we still come up short and

Chapter 4: Facing My Insecurities

even we, as parents, blame ourselves when they do the total opposite of what they were taught. We do all we can to try and get to the bottom of why our children misbehave and display inappropriate and unacceptable behavior. I believe in all our research, it's about who or what is influencing them as well as their decision to make wise choices.

I would hope that we are trying to develop healthy relationships with our children so that they can comfortably talk to us instead seeking others to talk to or find some other way to handle whatever may be troubling them. We know that more often than not, they will look for help outside of the home. There may be things going on inside of the home that causes the child to act out: a sudden or recent loss of a loved one, pressure from peers at school, etc.

We, as parents, have a responsibility and the children need to know that they, too, have a responsibility. Some of us may not have had a good example, so that role may be difficult. I knew that there were some things I just wouldn't do as a parent because of my own experiences. I don't think we necessarily have to raise our children the way we were raised. We take what works and learn along the way. Things are certainly different now and times have changed. I knew I was going to need some help raising my children and that help was going to come from God. I wanted my children to be able to rely on someone and trust in someone a whole lot stronger than me. They needed to be able to pray and get ahold of God for themselves in case I couldn't help.

Chapter Five
WE WERE CREATED FOR LOVE

We're all created to be in relationships with one another. There's a saying that no man is an island. Genesis 1:27-28 says, "So God created man in His own image, in the image of God He created him; male and female He created them. Then the Lord said it wasn't good for man to be alone; I will make him a helper fit for him." We all need someone with whom we can talk and relate.

In order to have a healthy relationship we must realize that Christ is the foundation on which we are to build any relationship. He should be in the center and everything else should revolve around Him. When God created the creatures of the land and sea—the fish and all of the "creeping things"—man was alone. God said it wasn't good that man was alone, so He created someone that Adam could identify with.

Those of you that have studied the Bible may be familiar with the story in Numbers 22:22-33 where God opened the mouth of a donkey to speak to its owner about how he was mistreating him. This reminds me of the movie Dr. Doolittle. I think it's funny that there's nothing new under the sun. The donkey was letting his owner know that he didn't deserve to be treated the way he was treating him considering their relationship.

A healthy relationship thrives off of respect. Respect, in my opinion, is an absolute must. We must be willing to be respectful toward one another no matter how much their beliefs or lifestyles may differ from ours. I also believe that we are obligated to show respect. The saying goes, "To get respect it takes respect." Sometimes not reacting to someone being disrespectful shows them their true self and may bring an awareness that leads to change.

There are all types of relationships where we must interact with one another, for example, employer and employee, co-worker and co-worker, etc. In this type of setting respect can be taken for granted. I often think if the employer builds rapport with their employees, establishes professionalism, and has rules stating that whether we have a relationship outside

Chapter 5: We Were Created For Love

of work it's about company policies, procedures and performance, friendship can develop in the workplace; however, a healthy relationship won't expect special treatment nor put that boss or supervisor in a difficult position when it comes to taking disciplinary action when necessary.

Speaking of friendship, friends often observe each other's conduct and reputation. A friend should be someone in whom you can confide personal information we may not tell anyone else. We have the right to choose who we want to call our friends and in doing so we only hope we have made a good choice. Trust, loyalty, and honesty are some of the essential ingredients needed in order to maintain that type of relationship.

All relationships have what I call a Developmental Stage to determine how far it will go. I don't call everyone I interact with my friend; I have some I refer to as associates. I may see you out in passing and may even know a little bit about you; we might partake in some small talk, comment on each other's hair or outfit, and continue being courteous and kind, but we keep it moving and nothing is wrong with that.

A friend is someone you've grown fond of. You trust one another and you have each earned that trust and respect. Although you may not hang out or talk on a regular basis, you're there for each other and can tell one another the truth without getting offended—

well, you might, but you realize they didn't intend to hurt you.

Relationships require a certain level of trust, especially the very intimate ones. We learn how to trust at an early age. We learn as children from our parents. They show us affection through their hugs, kisses, protection, and care. However, I believe that this is another foundation for some to build other relationships on. When that relationship is broken as a child due to abuse, neglect, abandonment, etc., and if that child does not receive inner healing or get restored, this child will have a distorted view of what trust is and therefore won't know how to trust. He or she may not understand nor recognize their actions or know how to respond when someone is trying to show them love.

Trust and love sometimes come with a price tag that says, "as long as," instead of, "as is." 'What do you mean?' Well, I'm glad you asked. It means as long as you agree with me, tell me what I want to hear, and do what I want you to do on my terms, I'll trust you. "As is" means I love you as you are, although I may not always agree with you. We can't allow our friendships to be developed out of control or manipulation.

I stated earlier that trust, honesty, and loyalty are essential ingredients for a healthy relationship. I believe these work hand-in-hand. If I trust you then I must believe I can be honest with you, and if I am honest with you I must believe I can trust you enough to

Chapter 5: We Were Created For Love

tell you the truth, even if it may hurt. When you have an established relationship with someone, that person knows you have their best interest at heart. A healthy relationship means you must be trustworthy in order to be trusted. We must recognize that contrary to what we may believe, everybody needs somebody and we all need love.

We were all created from love, in love and out of love. 1 John 4:7 says, *"Beloved, let us love one another: for love is of God; and every one that loveth is born of God and knoweth God."* 1 John 4:11 says, *"Beloved, if God so loved us, we ought also to love one another. It is that love that sustains us and is keeping us alive."* John 3:16 says, *"For God so loved the world that He gave His only begotten son…"* I believe there is a strong need to be loved, as well as giving that love away, whether that love is for a person, a pet, or something else."

Chapter Six
The Foundation Of A Healthy Relationship

A FEW CHAPTERS BACK, I BRIEFLY DISCUSSED the developmental stage of relationships. This is the growth process that determines what the outcome of the relationship you're involved in will be. I often wonder whether many of us love our neighbor(s) as ourselves. "Thou shall love thy neighbor as thyself" (Leviticus 19:18). In my observation of people, I came to the conclusion that a whole lot of people don't like themselves based on the way they treat others. There may be some legitimate reasons why some people have treated others poorly. The trust may have been broken, or something painful and devastating may have happened that caused what was once a healthy relationship to go toxic or bad. But for any of us to have healthy relationships, we need hearts that are willing to forgive. We must put ourselves in the other person's shoes. *The fit may be tight, but forgiveness frees you from the discomfort; it allows you to let go of resentment, as well as frees the other person from the captivity of guilt they may not have even realized they were under.* I'm not assuming that any of this is easy, but a healthy relationship is possible and we can have it.

We are spiritual beings who live in a body that is home to a soul. The spirit man is fed by the word of God. The soul is fed by love: this is where our will, intellect, and emotions dwell. Our body is fed with food. In order to maintain a healthy relationship, everything needs to be balanced properly. Just as the body needs to be nourished properly and exercised to stay healthy, so does a relationship. We know it takes discipline, time, and commitment to achieve the desired results. A healthy relationship requires being committed, taking time, having patience, and being understanding and considerate of one another's feelings. I also like to think obtaining a healthy relationship requires a sense of responsibility. Hmmmm! What am I saying? I am only responsible for how I treat you, not for how you treat me. Regardless of how rude, impolite, or inappropriate someone is acting toward me, I must choose

Chapter 6: The Foundation Of A Healthy Relationship

how I'm going to respond or if I need to respond at all. However, if I choose to respond or react, I must take responsibility for my actions. Those of us who confess to be Christians must walk with integrity, but do we have a moral responsibility as well? I tend to think it just feels good to be polite, kind, and respectful. A person could possibly be won over if enough people show them love.

 We owe it to ourselves to be responsible and deal with the issues that lay rooted below the surface, buried in our hearts. If we have experienced abuse (verbal or physical), rejection, betrayal, abandonment, etc. from an unhealthy relationship, often times we are left with the feeling of not being wanted or loved. The pain, guilt, shame, and resentment that we've suppressed leaves us emotionally scarred. Our emotions can be so damaged that our perception or our ability to process our thoughts about certain things gets distorted. We no longer know how to express ourselves in a healthy manner. Our failure to deal with these issues can cause our emotions to spiral out of control and escalate to the point that our behavior becomes self-destructive as well as damaging to others. We must recognize when we need to seek professional help. In maintaining a healthy relationship, we must first be healthy ourselves. We all have needs, and when those needs are neglected or not appropriately met, we may suffer mental anguish and find it difficult to function and complete our daily chores. Whenever we feel exhausted and drained of all energy and strength to the point that we can't finish even the simplest tasks, this is when professional counseling is necessary.

A healthy relationship involves being able to distinguish what type of relationship is to be established. We are accountable to one another in making sure the other person has a clear understanding of what to expect. There are boundaries and guidelines to consider. A friendship might be mistaken for something that it's not if the individuals don't make it plain. I'm kind of cautious about letting someone label me as their best friend. Their expectations of what they may consider that to be could be more demanding and may include some unrealistic terms I refuse to agree with. Establishing a healthy relationship doesn't mean we have to live up to someone else's expectation of us; trying to do so can and will cause unnecessary stress. We all know about the effects that stress can have on our health. I believe if we have boundaries and guidelines, it will help us to eliminate stress.

Depending on the type of relationship, the people in that relationship must know what's acceptable and what is not. I call this a healthy start. You are giving those involved an opportunity to avoid anything that could be hurtful and disruptive to the relationship. Communication is vitally important to any relationship. We must, to the best of our ability, make sure the person with whom we choose to be in a relationship has an understanding and that we are on the same page. *It is possible to be on the same page but in the wrong paragraph so-to-speak.*

I've not only seen it, but I've experienced certain situations where things can complicate or ruin a relationship; for example, loaning large sums of money or moving in with a friend. I would say that in this case, one has to be absolutely certain by using judgment, which could mean saying no. It's okay not to agree to something you are not comfortable with in order to salvage the friendship or keep the relationship healthy. I mentioned having boundaries and guidelines which I feel is necessary, especially with those of the opposite sex. Friends that are opposite in gender (or now-a-days, the same gender) should not make sexual comments or display inappropriate behavior toward one another. We joke around and play it off as 'I was just kidding.' The individuals may know it's not what it looks like, but what about someone else witnessing you grabbing or brushing up against that person? You don't want your conduct to be misleading nor make the other person feel uncomfortable like you are taking them for granted.

Setting boundaries and guidelines puts something in place to try and help prevent something from happening against our will. We do this to make sure we are not inviting or giving someone an opportunity to misuse that type of aggression in the wrong way.

I seem to be addressing a lot about friendships—speaking of which, true friends don't sleep with their best friend's significant other. In my opinion that happens far more often than it should. Why? I'm not so sure there's just one answer or explanation. We can't forget about the trust, loyalty, and honesty I mentioned as a necessary requirement for calling someone a friend. There have been case studies that found the most successful marriages were those that started out as a friendship. We sometimes make the mistake of turning a really good friendship into an intimate relationship only to realize we were better off as friends. In the most intimate relationships, I believe love is at the top of the list.

There are also relationships where individuals share mutual friends. Consider this story: Sheila and Warren are a couple who have been dating. They are out and about when Warren suddenly runs into his ex, Trisha. They agreed to go their separate ways after two years. "Hey Trisha!" Warren says, "This is Sheila. Sheila, Trisha!" Trisha thinks she recognizes Sheila, but Sheila isn't sure she remembers Trisha.

Trisha remembers, "Ohhh yeah, at the salon." Sheila wasn't a regular client, so she only vaguely remembered. Sean, who is Warren's homie, happens to be driving through town and spots them.

Sean pulls up and says, "What's up, Warren, my

Chapter 6: The Foundation Of A Healthy Relationship

man!" Warren turns to respond as Sean is getting out of the car. The two shake hands and brush shoulders. Warren asks what Sean has been up to and Sean says not much.

Then Sean says, "Hi Trisha and Sheila, right?" Warren then suggests they all get together that Friday since it's been a while. Everyone agrees. Sean asked Trisha if it would be okay if he picked her up instead of driving in separate cars. Trisha said that's fine.

"Great," Sean and Warren said, "can't wait." Then they all drove off.

On Friday, they all drive into the parking lot of a really classy restaurant. Sheila notices a live band playing and she comments on how nice the music sounds. The hostess comes over to greet them and seats them at their table, shortly thereafter a waitress shows up. "Hi! I'm Melinda! I'll get your drinks and some appetizers if you are ready." Once they place their orders the waitress leaves and Warren makes eye contact with his ex, Trisha. He thought to himself, 'She looks great!' He begins to wonder if he had made a mistake when he suggested that they go their separate ways.

Trisha really didn't know Sean very well, but Sean knew of her from the times Warren would bring her up after they separated a few months back. Sean did have a conversation with her while driving over to the restaurant. It was just small talk. He didn't want her to feel uncomfortable. Warren was quite the ladies' man, although he and Trisha did try to make things work.

Sean and Trisha are getting along pretty well and he's enjoying the attention. Sean and Warren never discussed or made any vows not to mess around with each other's ex-women. The vibes are becoming intense and Sean is not comfortable with what's happening. Warren seems to be a little agitated and Sheila is picking up on it and starts to wonder what's really going on. They somehow manage to shut it down and refocus on having a good time, getting rid of the awkwardness that was trying to ruin their evening.

The waitress returns with the drinks, and as she's sitting them down on the table, she says, "I'll be back with the rest of your orders." The ladies take a few sips of their drinks and decide to go to the ladies room.

They're washing their hands and Sheila says to Trisha, "If you don't mind me asking, what happened that you and Warren broke it off?" Trisha politely explained that with their work schedules and his side jobs, the relationship began to suffer from a lack of commitment, so they came to a mutual agreement to end the relationship.

"I really hope it works out for you," Trisha said, "he's a nice guy."

Meanwhile, Sean and Warren are chillin' at the table. Warren says to Sean, "You and Trisha seem to be hitting it off."

Chapter 6: The Foundation Of A Healthy Relationship

Sean says, "She seems like a fun, loving person. What happened?"

Warren's responds with, "She is, man. It's too much to get into. The problem may have been me along with working a lot. I won't have a problem if you decide you would like to date her."

Sean says, "Really! I wouldn't do that…nahhhh, man. I don't get down like that. Besides, we are partners. Even if Trisha would agree to it, that would be a little weird, awk….ward!" They see the ladies coming back and Sean gives Warren a bit of advice, saying, "Sheila seems to be a great fit as well, don't blow it again."

I said all that to say this concerning friends not sleeping or going out with their best friend's lady or man: the moral of the story is Sean may have been attracted to Trisha, but his relationship with his homie and longtime friend was more valuable to him. He didn't want to risk getting involved even though Warren said he didn't mind. Sean resisted the temptation and stayed true, not only to his friend, but to his own morals and standards. Some things we just should not do! You can also see in this mini story some of the ingredients I stated before that are essential to having a healthy relationship.

There may have been times when you've been in the company of friends at a social gathering and someone makes an inappropriate comment, touching you or giving you a wink even though they're already engaged or married. You can't allow yourself to be in the company of that person when others are not present. You also have the right to confront that individual and assure them that if it doesn't stop, you will let their significant other know what they did. Hopefully that nips it right in the bud. *We can't flirt with temptation or the thought of it.* We are only inviting trouble when we do. 1 Corinthians 10:13 says, *"No temptation has overtaken you. God will not allow you to be tempted beyond what you are able, but with the temptation will also make a way of escape that you may be able to bear it."* The truth be told, we're not trying to escape sometimes.

I believe that there are some lines that shouldn't be crossed such as sleeping with family members' or your friends' man or woman, especially if you're married. It is only when you give in that we say things like 'It just happened' or 'I didn't mean for it to go that far,' usually after the fact. This is the purpose for those boundaries and guidelines being put into place. We can be inconsiderate and selfish with our actions as well as our attitude. We must have some sense of self control over that which belongs to someone else. We'll discuss a little later about marriages and cheating.

Friendships between females are a little more complex; for example, there may be a few ladies who you are friends with and really close to, but those same

Chapter 6: The Foundation Of A Healthy Relationship

ladies have another circle of friends they hang out with as well. You know of them, but you don't kick it with them or hang with them like that. But, say, for instance, you all end up out one night at a party. You are having an interesting conversation when one of the other ladies decides to bring up some very sensitive and personal information that you had confided in someone you believed was your best friend. The look of devastation on your face causes your friend to apologize as you are grabbing your things and trying to leave. We tend to take situations such as this and use it against one another without being considerate of the other person's feelings. Trust, again, becomes an issue, because as women we can get into that catty, jealous, stab-you-in-the-back mess. I think women are a little more vocal and expressive than men. It can be a relationship with friends or an intimate relationship, but once that trust has been broken it's very hard to trust again. We develop defense mechanisms as a way of guarding and protecting our hearts.

Proverbs 4:23 says, *"Guard your heart with all diligence, for out of it springs the issues of life."* At some point, we began to take this scripture out of context. We build walls and we pull back, not allowing anyone to get too close to us. We isolate ourselves which only leads to loneliness. We deny anyone who may be a potential candidate for companionship or a healthy relationship. We cover up our true feelings by hiding behind this tough exterior, while that wounded and hurt person trapped within ourselves is screaming. We're unable to express freely what it is we really want because we're too afraid of being hurt again. *Our past experiences cause us to view relationships like traffic lights and signs; yield, proceed with caution, move slowly; yellow light—prepare to stop in case of a sudden red light indicating red flags which say "stop"; then the green light means it's safe to proceed, you can go, it's all good.* You can be off to a good start and for some reason begin thinking that this is too good to be true. The very things we want from the relationship—love, trust, honesty, commitment and acceptance—seem to be there. We allow the fear of being hurt to cause us to deliberately sabotage the relationship.

Men who've been hurt, from my observation and experience, ya'll be on some other stuff. Some of you are very prideful, arrogant, and afraid of being real. You never show your sensitive side, trying to be hard and cool, yet defensive. You have this need to prove your point as a man instead of being honest about the rejection you have had to deal with from your pasts, whether it was from a parent, an ex, or someone else. The frustration from a lack of accomplishments, feelings of inadequacy, and being disappointed with your own expectations of yourself and others can cause you to manipulate and play mind games. No one has the right to play with people's emotions. I believe as a re-

Chapter 6: The Foundation Of A Healthy Relationship

sult of unresolved issues that *hurt people* hurt people.

People who have made the choice to be in an intimate relationship with someone for years without getting married may appear like they're committed to one another for the most part; however, when one of them decides to flirt and have a wandering eye, they think it's okay until they're caught. There is a difference between looking and lusting: looking says he or she is attractive, but lusting says, 'Hmmmm, I wouldn't mind getting it on with him or her!' This type of disrespect only reveals how much this person means to you and it could also ruin any possibility of taking your relationship to another level.

Women are just as guilty when it comes to infidelity and flirting. We misuse our bodies and beauty to entice and seduce. Though we are not as easily exposed as men are, that doesn't necessarily mean men cheat more than women. I think we just hide it better. It has been said that women tease and flirt more than men. I see nothing wrong with innocently flirting with someone if you're interested and you are both single.

I think we stereotype men as dogs or they're labeled as a ladies man based on our personal experience with them or their reputation. We, as women, have also been labeled gold diggers or high maintenance. In order to properly assess and evaluate a relationship, we have to be true to ourselves in defining our motives for wanting to start a relationship with someone.

I'd say from a biblical perspective that this type of conduct as a Christian is unacceptable; however, sexual immorality for non-believers may be considered normal or expected. A healthy relationship is being able to use wisdom to do the right thing with every decision we make. We must be wise enough to think ahead as to who might get hurt and how many people could be affected by the decision. We have no way of really knowing to what degree or depth of pain we can cause someone. The person who feels they have been deceived, betrayed, or made a fool of, this person could suffer severe emotional trauma. They could have a nervous breakdown or even want to take their life. You're now left with the guilt and shame. For what? A few moments of pleasure and temporary relief and satisfaction brought on by infatuation and lust. The craving to feed the desire for that which belongs to someone else can never be fulfilled. You want to break it off but you can't because now you're emotionally attached, so you continue until you eventually get caught or you realize that it's just not worth it. It appears that one gender takes more heat in situations like these because they're more easily stereotyped. The truth of the matter is sometimes we convince ourselves to believe the other person really cared for us, whether married, separated, or just dating. It's all about respecting what you have and what you're trying to build with someone.

How many of us that are married have been

asked, "Are you married?" and your response was yes. But the next thing that came out of their mouth was, "Are you happy?" I'm not sure whether we should respond, walk away, or tell them it's none of their business. But I know that we shouldn't open a door that gives that person an opportunity to plant a seed. You may be experiencing some challenges in your marriage, but it's not the time to downplay or devalue the relationship by inviting outside interferences.

I have also had conversations with some Christian men, especially those who hold leadership roles in the church, which I've found very disturbing. They think it's okay to be sexually involved. They'll say, 'No one has to know but us.' A man and woman desiring each other, those are natural feelings that God gave us. When they say things like that, there's only one thing to do: Run!!!

Our parents taught us as children to respect our elders and those in authority. We see today that anyone—coaches, teachers, Boy Scout Leaders, clergy, and even family members—can be violators. I often wonder if it's easier for the ones we look up to or trust to violate us because of that trust. They're convinced they'll be the least likely to be suspected. I've heard it said before that *the most dangerous person is the predator of the heart. They will not only sin with you, but against you.* I'm not saying don't trust anyone, just be careful who you trust and what you entrust them with.

You Can Have It! It's Possible! Healthy Relationships

Chapter Seven
BEFORE YOU JUMP BACK IN

*I*N OUR PURSUIT FOR A MEANINGFUL AND healthy relationship, no matter what type, we have to be sure we don't have an unrealistic view of what that ideal person should look like or be. It's okay to have a preference, of course, as long as we are aware that some of those things could change after you've been together for some years. *We sometimes look for a mate like we are looking for a dream house with all the amenities.* In fact, we make statements like 'I'm on [or off] the market.' We must learn how to date, have fun, be friends, and just enjoy the company of each other without having the mindset that the other person will be our life partner. If you already have a list of criteria, you begin to develop these preconceived notions after a few months of dating. If you have not been able to heal from past relationships, you may have trigger points that remind you of what hurt you before and you'll allow this to interfere with what might possibly be a committed healthy relationship.

I tend to think Christian dating is different. We can't expect just a vibe or feeling of chemistry to be the sole determinant of whether or not a relationship is worth pursuing. You may not feel any of that, but does that mean there's no real connection just because those elements are not present? We must realize when we've been in toxic relationships, a time of healing and restoration is necessary. The painful and hurtful memories, over the top expectations, and false beliefs must now be downloaded and deleted. In other words, we may need to do a spiritual cleanse or detoxification in order to eliminate any parasites that could be lingering from previous relationships. Our systems could be infected with parasites of shame, guilt, low self-esteem, and embarrassment. The poison spreading throughout our bodies has us so self-absorbed and withdrawn that our minds begin to tell us not to trust anyone and to use others like we have been used. We become bitter and resentful toward men or vice versa and then we're unable to entertain the possibility of beginning a genuine relationship with someone. We can get so bad that our health starts to spiral out of control so that we are now

CHAPTER 7: BEFORE YOU JUMP BACK IN

in need of not only a 911 call, but a spiritual IV as well so we can get our strength and courage back. Once we are restored, we finally understand who we are and whose we are. We are now on our way to full recovery.

I used to wonder why certain men were attracted to me. I would ask myself, 'Do I have some invisible neon sign that only jerks can see?!' I was praying one day and I asked the Holy Spirit why this was, and deep as this may sound, the Holy Spirit said to me, "Because you allowed yourself to interact with those type of men, the spirit that was on them has attached itself to you and like a magnet they're drawn to you." WOW!! That made sense to me. Contrary to what we may believe we're more spirit than anything. I, of course, wanted to know what I needed to do. I went through a period of sanctification and consecration. Hallelujah! I haven't been approached by that type of man ever since. Heck, I haven't been really approached by any men (LOL)! I'm good with that. I don't have to settle for an unhealthy relationship just to feel loved or accepted. I don't want to take the chance of being abused, unappreciated, and not treated as the priceless, precious jewel that God has created me to be. I believe that desire will be fulfilled when the time is right. Our preference sometimes get distorted by the types of relationships we have been involved in. For instance, say you like the bad boy type. He appears to be tough, strong, and like he will protect you at all costs, but the flip side of that might be he's very abusive verbally and physically. You feel safe and protected when you're together, but what happens when he snaps? Now, the one you actually need protection from is him. We somehow develop this false sense of security, convincing ourselves that it won't happen again, that it was just an isolated incident. But it happened. Don't live in denial.

I mentioned before that if we experience neglect, abuse and abandonment as children, we learn to tolerate this kind of treatment. I think for some, no matter how bad an individual is being treated, that person may think it's easier to stay involved in a relationship. They'd rather cling to that little bit of attention as chaotic and abusive as it may be than be alone. The fear of abandonment gets to be overwhelming and they become afraid to escape. It is easy to be deceived into thinking it will get better.

The need to be loved and accepted can sometimes becloud our vision, making us believe that in order to fit in or belong this means we must do whatever it takes. A healthy relationship accepts people the way they are and allows them to grow and mature at their own pace. We don't need to try and change someone, nor do we need to become co-dependent and enablers of other people's issues. We shouldn't feel obligated to accept someone else trying to control us to the point that we lose ourselves and lose touch with our family and friends.

I often wonder how many of us put detainers on our relationships, holding the other person captive to our unreasonable terms and conditions until we feel like they've met the necessary requirements or demands in order to be set free?

We seem to have created a shortage of men for women who are trying to have a meaningful relationship. There are women who lack self-esteem. They don't mind working, supporting the household; and the only thing the man has to do is be at home, maybe cook, use your car whenever he wants, or if he has car, take you to work, hang out all day until it's time to pick you up from work for which he arrives late; you buy his clothes and any the other things he may want. You finally realize that this relationship is not beneficial or healthy. You become fed up and tired of his lack of motivation or interest to contribute to this so-called relationship you thought you had. So you end the relationship and he's off to the next "victim," some young lady with low or no self-esteem at all. We, as women, sometimes fool ourselves into thinking that if we could have a man with a perfect physique in our lives, we would somehow be complete. But in a committed relationship such as a marriage, *we don't complete one another, we compliment and enhance one another.*

Women are not exempt. Those of us who've had a decent man who works, helps provide, helps out around the house, contributes financially, likes spending time at home with us, and doesn't complain when we want to hang out with our girlfriends have ruined it. There we go! We start being disrespectful and nagging. All of a sudden, he doesn't make enough money to handle your compulsive shopping habits, etc. If we continue to create relationships like these, how can we stop this vicious cycle? These men and women should realize they don't have to settle for an unhealthy relationship just to say they have someone, which often results in domestic violence. We must care enough to view ourselves in the light of God and through His eyes. It is easy to meditate on the negative words and pain that was caused to you as a result of being in a unhealthy relationship. The memories from all the hurt that floods our minds sometimes make it very difficult to escape the past.

In order to become healthy again, we must look to the Wonderful Counselor and seek His guidance and counsel. God is the only one we need to validate us. We must erase all of the negative things people have said and done to us and replace them with positive, encouraging, and uplifting words. Psalms 139:13, 14 says, *"You formed me in my inwards parts; you covered me in my mother's womb. I will praise you for I am fearfully and wonderfully made."*

I have learned some valuable and hard lessons through my many experiences. I'm grateful for my

Chapter 7: Before You Jump Back In

journey thus far. I believe my relationship with God, along with the guidance of my parents, is what helped sustain me when I was going through some very challenging and difficult times in my life. I've come to understand God loves me completely, and He's the one that validates me. I now know I don't need to get involved in unhealthy relationships or seek approval and acceptance at any cost. We don't have to tolerate abuse and be so overwhelmed with guilt and shame that we accept whatever is presented to us. We become so obsessed with what we didn't get that our vision becomes marred by our pain and suffering. We fail to see that what appeared to be love was only a disguise. God is the epitome of genuine and true love and this love should reflect in the lives of those who know Him and have a relationship with Him because this love dwells in them.

I was a single mom at eighteen and later married at the age of twenty-seven. I divorced in 2005. I enjoy where I am in this phase of my life. I love being involved in ministry. I enjoy traveling and spending time with my grandchildren. Yes, I am open to a healthy relationship, but that's not my main focus at the moment.

Healthy relationships may seem impossible because they require commitment and a willingness to give of one's self. We can't enter a relationship with ulterior motives and hidden agendas. We can't expect to gain and benefit without contributing. We must be careful with all of the ways we can throw off, offend, betray, deceive, and embarrass one another. Social media and other technologies have made it more difficult for us to interact on a personal level. We still need to make and take time to sit face-to-face and enjoy one another's presence every now and then.

I want you to remember that Christ is the perfect example of a healthy relationship. He makes it so that with Him, there's no need to pretend, go out of your way, go along with, or be overly nice or aggressive, etc. Christ loves us the way we are. Likewise, in a healthy relationship, you should have the freedom to be you—your authentic self. So, realize that...YOU CAN HAVE IT! IT'S POSSIBLE! You can experience authentic love, and a healthy relationship! But it starts with inner healing and an understanding from the Bible of the foundation of a healthy relationship.

ABOUT THE AUTHOR

Cynthia "Faye" Hayes Simpson is a speaker, writer, and author. She is an ordained Evangelist and a former Elder. Faye organized Youth Going Forth. She is also the founder of Personal Touch Women's Ministry (now called W.O.M.B.S.).

Cynthia's faithfulness to work as the Department Head of Evangelism and the Prison Ministry is well known to those she serves with. Working to serve others in this capacity is a passion of hers which fuels her.

Cynthia continues to write. Writing is a passion of hers. She loves to write about different life's topics and she loves to write poetry. She is also a business woman and a devoted mother and grandmother.

To contact the author, go to:
cfsimpson46@yahoo.com
Facebook: Faye Hayes Simpson
Linked In: Faye Simpson
Instagram: FayeSimp78

www.ingramcontent.com/pod-product-compliance
Lightning Source LLC
Chambersburg PA
CBHW052113070526
44584CB00017B/2468